COPYRIGHT

Copyright © 2018 by Desire Akoda
All rights reserved. No part of this publication may be reproduced, distributed, or transmitted in any form or by any means, including photocopying, recording, or other electronic or mechanical methods, without the prior written permission of the publisher, except in the case of brief quotations embodied in critical reviews and certain other noncommercial uses permitted by copyright law. For permission requests, write to the publisher, addressed "Attention: Permissions Coordinator," at the information below.

Ordering Information:
Available at www.weareaurum.com and www.amazon.com
Quantity sales. Special discounts are available on quantity purchases by corporations, associations, and others. For details, contact the publisher at the address above.
Orders by U.S. trade bookstores and wholesalers. Please visit www.weareaurum.com.
Printed in the United States of America

Table of Content

COPYRIGHT

Table of Content

Acknowledgments

What is Social Media?

Step 1

Step 2

Step 3

Step 4

Step 5

Acknowledgments

My mother Marie, one of the strongest women on this planet. Most people would have given up when faced with all the setbacks in life, but she continues to strive for greatness.

Cairo - The lady of many talents. Cairo has been tremendous support for me. I would not have been able to write this book without her support.

Sonia Jennings - My mentor who always inspires me day by day. I always wanted to write a book and publish it. She has shown me the ropes and provided me with all the necessary resources to reach my "author" goals.

Warren Brown - The man that introduced me to all of the wonderful things facebook had to offer brands and empowered me to embark on this wonderful entrepreneurial journey. He flew me and a friend out to Miami and showed me secrets that he was using to leverage these tools and make at minimum $1000/day for his company.

What is Social Media?

When we mention social media, most people break that down as Social and others as Media. When people see the word social, they all of a sudden think that it is all about socializing. Social media seems taboo to certain people because it is seen as a place to go and waste time, gossip or even a place to escape from reality. Others stay away from it because of the amount of personal information one may publicize to the whole world. Well, what we see is a place to connect with people. It is not all about socializing. The denotation of the word social from Websters dictionary is an adjective "relating to society or its organization". Media is the main means of mass communication. Media is just an instrument to connect or relate to society and have an endless reach.

Social media has a few advantages.

1. You can share information with someone all the way across the earth and in some way keep the anonymity of both parties.
2. It is accessible to anyone 24/7, 365 days.
3. There are no limitations when it comes down to geography. You can connect with someone on the other side of the world.
4. It doesn't cost you anything extra. All you need is an internet connection.

   These same aspects that I have listed above to make social media a positive force in our daily lives but could also be very dangerous to us at the same time. The same information we make public could be seen by some anonymous people who could attempt to ruin one's image or steal personal information from us. Nowadays it is very hard to trust people or companies that are providing services to keep us and our information secure. A number of these same people are the ones that are attacking us anonymously so we would seek their services. For example most viruses are created by companies that create antivirus software to infiltrate your system which makes you purchase their software. So the best thing one should do is learn about the internet and know what information to not disclose.

Kids in schools use social media to bully each other every day. It is a place where you can see all forms of bullying administered by all ages. It is also a great source of news but in this era, we have what you call "fake news". Social media is an open source, peer to peer platform so the information published could be from anyone. If the news is not coming from a reliable source, then make sure you fact check everything. It is not expensive so anyone could get their hands on this technology.

Social media isn't slowing down anytime soon. It has changed the way we do business today. With more and more people joining daily, I urge your business to take advantage now before it's too late. I'm not saying this because it is a new, trendy thing businesses are doing but because most of your customers are hanging out on different social media platforms and connecting with your competitors. Why not leverage sites like Facebook, Twitter, and Instagram to connect with potential customers.

With Facebook being the powerhouse of all social networks, It is growing faster than ever imagined. Recently, Facebook CEO appeared before Congress regarding allegations of Data Harvesting and Misuse. Facebook does not disclose anyone's sensitive information like social security number, or credit card information. That information could only be public if the user decided to put it on their public profile. I am no way, shape, or form an investigator. In my opinion, I believe that Facebook stores all the information that we publicize through our posts and pictures in a database. For example, if I make a post talking about my love for ice cream, then Facebook will store it and remember that I love ice cream. This database has information about what a person likes, consumes, reads and so on. With this information, they are able to do the market research, and market segmentation for businesses. If an ice cream company wants to sell more ice cream, with the help of Facebook they will find ice cream lovers like myself. They then sell this information to allow brands to run ads for a targeted audience.

I have told people that Facebook knows more about you than any member of your family does. Social media algorithms are getting smarter and smarter that soon enough they may be able to predict our next moves.

2 million businesses use Facebook advertisements to promote their products and services. In the 1st quarter of 2017 alone, It reached $9.16 billion in ad revenue. Like Chris Smoove always says "What maneuver could possibly be any smoother".

This is by far a more effective advertisement tool than the traditional print media, tv, or radio ads. Let me tell you how.

1. The ad rates are less expensive because you won't need to purchase paper or ink.
2. You can choose whichever audience to target so you won't need to spend money to reach people that are not interested in your product.
3. You are able to check your ad's performance, unlike the other advertisement tools.

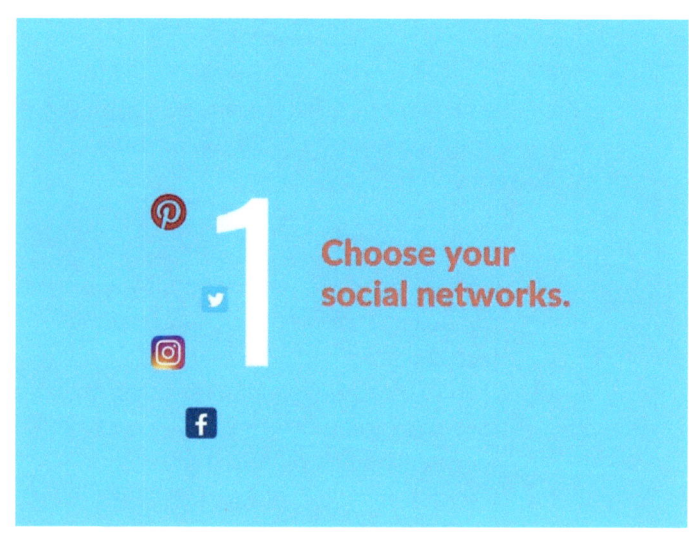

This step may seem frustrating to some because there's a good number of different social networks but trust me it's quite simple. I tell my clients this all the time. "You don't have to be on them all. Just select the ones that matter to your audience." You want to make your job as efficient as possible. Think of your audience as friends. You want to hang out at the same place as your friends. You must have time to be able to manage these social media accounts and the proper knowledge of creating content. I will elaborate more about content shortly. Most of my clients requested my services because as they are operating the vital parts of their business and they didn't have the time, knowledge or proper resources. If you don't have the time or resources, I would advise that you go get help from experts and check out www.weareaurum.com

2 Completely Fill out your Profile

Setting up the profile

- Show Professionalism
- Branding with logos, banners if needed
- Have a bio that will allow user to engage with you.

What have you done?

Your profile is basically your front door. It is what your audience will see before deciding if they should enter or not. Your goal is to make it so appealing that their sole option is to enter. Make sure your profile is completely filled out from top to bottom. Add a logo, banner, and even some pictures for branding purposes. This will make it look more professional and attract the user to your page. You must remain consistent with your visuals from top to bottom and across all social networking platforms. Your username should be consistent everywhere so it would be easier to be found. One great thing to do is a cross-platform promotion. This basically means that you are promoting your page on another platform. For example, you can leave a link of your Linkedin page on your Facebook profile. Include a written out bio to explain what your brand is about. Don't just tell them who you are but tell them what you have done and what you can offer them. Congratulations if you have completed this step. The job is not done yet.

Now you just need to revisit your profile once in a while and make updates if necessary.

3 Find your voice and tone

The next series of questions are needed to be answered by your brand as if it were a person. It basically is like you are creating a person. You are giving it a birthday, a name, an identity. It has a heart which is the operations aspect of the business. All it needs is a soul. Without a soul, we are no longer alive. You may now be thinking how am I supposed to give an entity or a non-living thing a soul. Before you can do that you need to imagine your brand as a human and answer these questions

1. What's your vision?
2. What do you stand for?
3. How do you relate to your audience?
4. How do you want to be viewed as?

Your brand's voice is the mission statement. Once you are able to find it, then you can find its tone. A tone is basically how you manage to implement the mission statement as you are operating your business. These are great things to consider. It shows your audience what you believe in and what you want to accomplish. If your beliefs align with that of your audience's, then they would be attached you your brand. If you have a brand that does not have a vision, then you are missing out on gaining loyal customers.

4 Pick your posting strategy

brand identity

- What should I Post
- How often should I post?
- When should I post

It Depends!!!!

My answer is always "it depends." Your audience will react differently each day due to many factors that are affecting their lives. They could be following other brands that offer the same product or service as you. In this case, if they see you post something similar to another brand, they may automatically consider the second one as spam and dismiss you. They could also see you as a content swiper. There are content swipers all over social media. That is why it is a good idea to watermark or put your brand image, name or logo on anything that you produce. Facebook and Instagram now have a new algorithm that no longer reveals our posts in chronological order. Posts are showing up in a random order. So you can post something that is happening that day and some members of your audience will only see it 2 or 3 days later. It hurts when this happens. A great way to avoid this is to post on several different platforms. The best way is to put reiterate to your audience the importance of turning on the post notifications so they will be notified as soon as you post. This way they will never again miss your posts.

Some people will not appreciate it if they only see mediocre posts all over their timeline for that day. One thing to avoid is posting too often. Aside to posting too often, don't post anything even if it does not concern your audience. Make sure it is something that will add some kind intrinsic value to their lives. Even if the post is not original content, make sure that you give the creator their credit. People invest a lot of time to put together great content for their audience.

I have a few people that I follow and I tend to get frustrated when they repost other content. Some of us only appreciate original content. So if you are going to start swiping other posts, you should alter it and add your own twist to it. Show your audience that you at least put some thought and time into it. On the next page, you will see how often you should be posting and what you should be posting. Some people just love visuals or inspirational quotes, so you just have to find the right audience. You may just need to have luck on your side or you can do it right and make sure your posts are unique and innovative. This is what attracts audiences and skyrockets engagement.

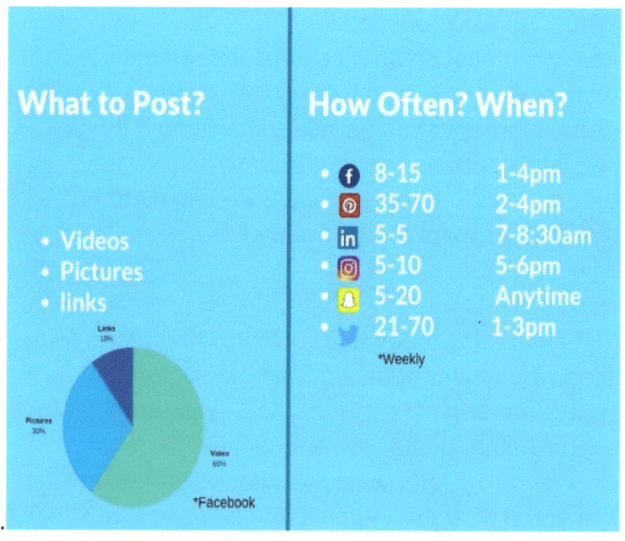

The social media engagement recipe

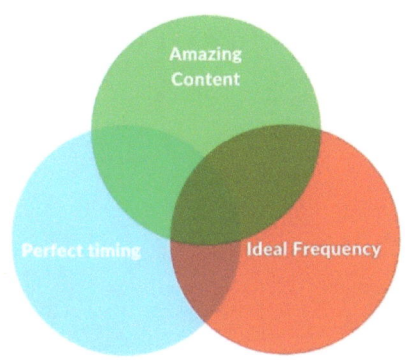

Content is very important because it can make or break your page. There must be a lot of value to what you post. Ideally, you need to be posting great quality videos because they tend to receive more engagement. When posting pictures, make sure it is planned cohesively with your branding, how it can relate to your audience, and how your audience can benefit from it. Posting times are based on the time that certain audiences are free or tend to browse social networks.

Linkedin: Linkedin is a networking website like facebook but concentrates more on the professional side of things. Most stuff done on there are work or career-related. Employers go on there to recruit and hire employees. While employees go on there to network with other professionals and get hired. It would be ideal to post any before your targeted audience goes to work and after they return from work.

Instagram: The best time to post on here is anytime after school or work but before bedtime. Usually tends to be between 5-10pm.

Snapchat keeps your stories published for 24 hours so you can post anytime you want.

You will have to consistently post and experiment to find out what works and what doesn't.

Here are a few examples of what you can post.

1. Run a promotion. (Sale, GIveaway, Contest)
2. Post a group challenge for your fans that are relevant to your products or services.
3. Share real customer testimonials (if they give you permission).
4. Make longer announcements that wouldn't fit in a tweet.
5. Post-behind-the-scenes pictures and introduce employees.
6. Share controversial or trending posts in your industry and start a debate in the comments.

7. Have a hashtag strategy. Consider incorporating trends such as #throwbackthursday (#tbt) or #fridayfun.

   Who does not love free stuff? We all do. So why not use this to maintain loyal followers. Contests and giveaways are a great method to capture leads and get people to engage with your brand. Stay updated with the news, media, pop culture especially within your market. Knowing the new trends will give you an edge. Allow your audience to see behind the scenes access to your world. Let them see how you make certain things or introduce them to the team that provides wonderful services. People love when they are included in exclusive content. Hashtags are used to grab the attention of the audience that does not follow you. It's like telling them "hey I'm over here check me out." Through my experience, I have noticed that hashtags on Facebook are ineffective. Twitter users may get annoyed if you put more than 2 hashtags. An Ideal amount of hashtags would be 10 but it is ok to put more on Instagram. Instagram is the platform that users tend to be unbothered by hashtags so feel free to go wild. The more you put, the bigger the audience you are able to reach. If you are intending to use a trendy hashtag, make sure that it is current and not outdated. Content-based hashtags tend to work well when the audience is encouraged to participate in a poll or a discussion.

5 Analyze and test

Once you have been posting for about 2 to 3 months, you can now start analyzing your work to figure out what works. Facebook Insights and Instagram Insights are a few free tools that you could use to analyze performance. Run at least a 3-month test when trying out new methods. Use your reports to see which changes need to be made.

what works best?

1. FOCUS ON YOUR CUSTOMERS Build your marketing strategy around your customers.	**2. BUILD YOUR BRAND'S STORY** Storytelling is one of the most powerful marketing tools.
3. UTILIZE CONTENT MARKETING Through creating quality content, you build customer trust.	**4. GET YOUR BUSINESS FOUND USING SEO** Search engines can connect you to new and relevant audiences.

These steps could be a great amount to handle while operating your business. To help alleviate some stress, contact professionals to manage your accounts for you. I hope that you now have the basic knowledge of setting up your page to maximize audience engagements. This here is the best way to get your brand in this social media space. I will go into what I believe works best. We all know the number one rule is to take care of your customer. Since your aim is to make sure they are pleased and return, you must then build and plan around them. Put yourself in their shoes to be able to apply the best procedures. Stories are very important. Stories are a form of entertainment. The individual gets detained, so they stop what they are doing to be able to soak up a story. That's why we watch movies, tv shows, and listen to music. That is also why you are reading this book. Connect with customers, people in your field. Learn about them and with them. Learn from their stories so you can use it as knowledge throughout your journey. Now you can tell your story and your experience to your audience. Show them the way by guiding them through their ups and downs. Use great tools like Snapchat and Instagram stories as your voice. Be consistent and schedule live streams so your audience could ask you questions on the spot.